Emily Luchetti

Ein Mottgel

SO WHO'S COUNTING?

THE LITTLE QUOTE BOOK ABOUT GROWING OLDER AND STILL KICKING ASS

ERIN McHUGH AND **EMILY LUCHETTI**

Andrews McMeel
PUBLISHING®

To Anne Burke Sadow
With love and thanks

CONTENTS

INTRODUCTION

We always thought of the '50s as Elvis and the postwar boom; the '60s as Woodstock, free love, and getting high; and the '70s as "The Me Decade," living the good life amid fondue, lava lamps, and disco madness. Now that we're *in* our 50s, 60s, and 70s, those numbers mean something else entirely: our age. They also mean Social Security, little aches and pains, and the gateway to our third act.

But really, things are just beginning to happen. We're healthier, we live longer than the generations before us; we have later-in-life careers; we go on dating websites; we're more engaged and travel farther.

Older is getting younger every day.

SO WHO'S COUNTING? is the book that proves it. It's an acknowledgment and affirmation of our journey, chock-full of inspiration, humor, and reminders that things are just beginning to happen.

The best is now.

ATTITUDE
IS
EVERYTHING

It's all in how you look at the world,
your life, your future.

Never say "no"
to adventures.

Always say "yes;"
otherwise, you'll lead
a very dull life.

Ian Fleming

Get busy living or get busy dying.

STEPHEN KING

I love life because what more is there?

ANTHONY HOPKINS

I want to be around a really long time. I want to be a thorn in the side of everything as long as possible.

PATTI SMITH

5

DON'T WAIT.
THE TIME WILL NEVER BE
JUST RIGHT.

NAPOLEON HILL

It isn't where
you come from,
it's where you're going
that counts.

ELLA FITZGERALD

The secret of long life is double careers. One to about age sixty, then another for the next thirty years.

DAVID OGILVY

I don't have any rules, because I'd only be breaking them.

IRIS APFEL

THE ONLY SAFE THING IS TO TAKE A CHANCE.

MIKE NICHOLS

I WAKE UP EVERY DAY
AND I THINK,
"I'M BREATHING!
IT'S A GOOD DAY."

EVE ENSLER

What I love best in life is new starts.

KARL LAGERFELD

FOR ME,
EVERY HOUR IS GRACE.

ELIE WIESEL

I'M THRILLED
TO DEATH
WITH LIFE.

JOHNNY CASH

I prefer to be a beautiful woman of my age than try desperately to look 30.

DEMI MOORE

YOU BLOWS WHO YOU IS.

LOUIS ARMSTRONG

At the end of every movie,
always I'm feeling,
"You're never going
to work again."
That's going to happen
one day, but I hope
I'm not alive.

Nobody looks good
when they get old . . .
but what the hell
can you do about it?
Nothing. So you may
as well ignore it as best
you can and just be
who you are.

GRACE SLICK

I NEED TO RETIRE
FROM RETIREMENT.

SANDRA DAY O'CONNOR

It's the rudest word in my dictionary, "retire." And "old" is another one. I don't allow that in my house. And being called "vintage." I don't want any of these old words. I like "enthusiastic."

JUDI DENCH

It is not true that people stop pursuing dreams because they grow old, they grow old because they stop pursuing dreams.

GABRIEL GARCÍA MÁRQUEZ

Getting old is a
fascinating thing.
The older you get,
the older you
want to get.

KEITH RICHARDS

AS OLD
AS YOU
FEEL

Age is a state of mind more than
a physical marker: Make sure you
approach life that way every day.

23

There is a fountain of youth: It is your mind, your talents, the creativity you bring to your life, and the lives of people you love. When you learn to tap this source, you will truly have defeated age.

SOPHIA LOREN

Everyone is the age of their heart.

GUATEMALAN PROVERB

I HAVE RETIRED, BUT IF
THERE IS ANYTHING
THAT WOULD KILL ME
IT IS TO WAKE UP
IN THE MORNING
NOT KNOWING
WHAT TO DO.

NELSON MANDELA

The trick is to age honestly and gracefully and make it look great, so that everyone looks forward to it.

EMMA THOMPSON

You may be old,
you may be in your
third act, but you
can still be vital and
sexual and funny.
Life isn't over.

JANE FONDA

Faster, faster, until the thrill of speed overcomes the fear of death.

HUNTER S. THOMPSON

THERE'S NOTHING
I WOULD RETIRE FOR,
SO I WON'T RETIRE.
I'LL JUST KEEP GOING
UNTIL I FALL OVER.

JAMES EARL JONES

People who say
you're just as
old as you feel
are all wrong,
fortunately.

RUSSELL BAKER

I figure
if I keep my
spirit in shape,
the bones will
take care of
themselves.

RITA MORENO

To me, age is always ten years older than I am.

There's a
part of you
that always
remains a child,
no matter how
mature you get,
how sophisticated
or weary.

BARBRA STREISAND

WE ARE ALWAYS
THE SAME AGE INSIDE.

GERTRUDE STEIN

In a dream, you are never eighty.

ANNE SEXTON

WE TURN NOT
OLDER WITH YEARS
BUT NEWER EVERY DAY.

EMILY DICKINSON

Youth has no age.

PABLO PICASSO

KEEP MOVING.

DICK VAN DYKE

I'm just too busy
living every day
to really spend a lot
of time thinking,
"Am I old?"
I'm this age. I am
in this moment
and in this life.

EMMYLOU HARRIS

I WANT TO
DIE YOUNG AT A
RIPE OLD AGE.

ASHLEY MONTAGU

SILVER LININGS

There are pluses to being older:
Let's focus on what those are and
make sure to enjoy them.

43

One of the few advantages to not being beautiful is that one usually gets better-looking as one gets older. I am, in fact, at this very moment gaining my looks.

NORA EPHRON

I didn't get old
on purpose,
it just happened.
If you're lucky,
it could happen
to you.

ANDY ROONEY

The great thing about getting older is that you don't lose all the other ages you've been.

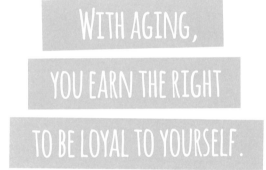

WITH AGING,
YOU EARN THE RIGHT
TO BE LOYAL TO YOURSELF.

FRANCES MCDORMAND

47

A sense
of freedom
is something that,
happily, comes
with age and life
experience.

DIANE KEATON

The longer I live, the more beautiful life becomes.

FRANK LLOYD WRIGHT

I look forward to
being older, when what
you look like becomes
less and less an issue
and what you are
is the point.

THE OLDER I GET, THE LESS
I KNOW. IT'S WONDERFUL—
IT MAKES THE WORLD
SO SPACIOUS.

SWAMI CHETANANANDA

Don't ever give up on life. Life can be so beautiful, especially after you've spent a lot of time with it.

YOKO ONO

I'm too old to do things by half.

LOU REED

I'm at the age where I don't have to kiss arse or play nice!

SHARON OSBOURNE

I HAVE REACHED AN AGE
WHEN, IF SOMEONE
TELLS ME TO WEAR SOCKS,
I DON'T HAVE TO.

ALBERT EINSTEIN

Aging is not lost youth but a new stage of opportunity and strength.

To be old
can be glorious
if one has
not unlearned
how to begin.

MARTIN BUBER

Ah, well, perhaps one has to be very old before one learns how to be amused rather than shocked.

PEARL S. BUCK

In youth
we learn,
in age we
understand.

MARIE VON EBNER-ESCHENBACH

OLD AGE AND TREACHERY
WILL ALWAYS BEAT
YOUTH AND EXUBERANCE.

DAVID MAMET

WISD**O**M OF
THE **A**GE

One of the things we have over the young
is experience and perspective. Our knowledge
is what makes us, well, superior!

AGE IS OF NO IMPORTANCE UNLESS YOU ARE A CHEESE.

LUIS BUÑUEL

I enjoy life
when things
are happening.
I don't care if
it's good things
or bad things.
That means
you're alive.

JOAN RIVERS

The minute that you're not learning I believe you're dead.

JACK NICHOLSON

It took me quite
a long time
to develop a voice,
and now that
I have it, I am not
going to be silent.

MADELEINE ALBRIGHT

There is only
one map to the
journey of life,
and it lives within
your heart.

WILLIE NELSON

A finished person is a boring person.

ANNA QUINDLEN

Maybe all one can do
is hope to end up with
the right regrets.

ARTHUR MILLER

When you're 16,
30 seems ancient.
When you're 30,
45 seems ancient.
When you're 45,
60 seems ancient.
When you're 60,
nothing seems ancient.

HELEN MIRREN

LIFE MOVES PRETTY FAST. IF YOU DON'T STOP AND LOOK AROUND ONCE IN A WHILE, YOU COULD MISS IT.

JOHN HUGHES

70

LOOK WHAT YOU'VE
ALREADY COME THROUGH!
DON'T DENY IT.
SAY I'M STRONGER THAN
I THOUGHT I WAS.

MAYA ANGELOU

A man who
views the world
the same
at fifty
as he did
at twenty
has wasted
thirty years
of his life.

MUHAMMAD ALI

We are who
we're going to be
when we're
very old, and
when we're
very old we are
who we were
when we were 8.

MERYL STREEP

Youth cannot know how age thinks and feels. But old men are guilty if they forget what it was to be young.

J. K. ROWLING

Find something
you're passionate
about and stay
tremendously
interested in it.

JULIA CHILD

Just celebrate
the life you had,
not the life you
could have had.

MAGIC JOHNSON

THE OLDER YOU GET, THE FEWER THINGS IT SEEMS TOO LATE TO DO.

ROBERT BREAULT

LAUGHTER: THE BEST PRESCRIPTION

Without a sense of humor, life simply isn't as much fun. You need a daily dose.

I love living.
I have some problems
with my life, but living
is the best thing they've
come up with so far.

NEIL SIMON

I INTEND TO LIVE FOREVER OR DIE TRYING.

GROUCHO MARX

I'M NOW AT THE AGE
WHERE I'VE GOT TO PROVE
THAT I'M JUST AS GOOD
AS I NEVER WAS.

REX HARRISON

I look to the future
because that's
where I'm going
to spend the
rest of my life.

GEORGE BURNS

Just remember,
when you're
over the hill,
you begin to
pick up speed.

CHARLES M. SCHULZ

Never ask anyone over 70 how they feel. They'll tell you.

BARBARA BUSH

THE MORE
I PRACTICE,
THE LUCKIER
I GET.

ARNOLD PALMER

I FIND IT HARDER AND
HARDER EVERY DAY TO LIVE
UP TO MY BLUE CHINA.

OSCAR WILDE

I'M GOING TO TO LIVE TILL I DIE.

FRANK SINATRA

88

After thirty, a body has a mind of its own.

BETTE MIDLER

IF I'D KNOWN
I WAS GOING TO
LIVE THIS LONG,
I'D HAVE TAKEN BETTER
CARE OF MYSELF.

EUBIE BLAKE

If you don't know where you are going, you might end up somewhere else.

YOGI BERRA

If I had to live my life again, I'd make all the same mistakes, only sooner.

HAPPINESS IS NOTHING MORE THAN GOOD HEALTH AND A BAD MEMORY.

ALBERT SCHWEITZER

You're never too old
to become younger.

MAE WEST

SMART AGING

We're still here. Let's not waste time.
It's all about the things we like to do
that bring us real joy.

As soon as you feel too old to do a thing, do it.

MARGARET DELAND

I never feel age . . .
If you have
creative work,
you don't have
age or time.

LOUISE NEVELSON

I am learning all the time. The tombstone will be my diploma.

EARTHA KITT

Old age, believe me,
is a good and
pleasant thing.
It is true you are
gently shouldered off
the stage, but then
you are given such a
comfortable front stall
as spectator.

CONFUCIUS

If you always do
what interests you,
at least one person
is pleased.

KATHARINE HEPBURN

The secret to living
well and longer is:
Eat half, walk double,
laugh triple, and love
without measure.

TIBETAN PROVERB

I JUST DON'T HAVE TIME TO GET OLD.

DOLLY PARTON

I don't want
to get to the end
of my life and
find that I lived
just the length of it.
I want to have
lived the width
as well.

DIANE ACKERMAN

When I am old and gray,
I want to have a house by
the sea. And paint. With
a lot of wonderful chums,
good music, and booze
around. And a damn good
kitchen to cook in.

At my age, in this
still hierarchical time,
people often ask me if
I'm "passing the torch."
I explain that I'm
keeping my torch,
thank you very much—
and I'm using it to light
the torches of others.

GLORIA STEINEM

SOMEBODY WHO CAN
RECKON WITH THE PAST,
WHO CAN LIVE WITH THE
PAST IN THE PRESENT,
AND MOVE TOWARD
THE FUTURE—
THAT'S FABULOUS.

BRUCE SPRINGSTEEN

I choose
to fill my days
with what I'm
passionate about,
and live
with purpose.

ANN CURRY

Nature gives
you the face you
have at twenty;
it is up to you
to merit the face
you have at fifty.

COCO CHANEL

WITH MIRTH AND LAUGHTER LET OLD WRINKLES COME.

WILLIAM SHAKESPEARE

Instructions for living a life. Pay attention. Be astonished. Tell about it.

Life is short.
Kiss slowly,
laugh insanely,
love truly,
and
forgive quickly.

PAULO COELHO

111

LIFE
LESSONS

A lot has happened along the way.
What we learn is what inspires our path.

I've been absolutely terrified every moment of my life—and I've never let it keep me from doing a single thing I wanted to do.

You go through phases.
You have to reinvent reasons
for playing, and one year's
answer might not do
for another.

YO-YO MA

THE ROAD IS LIFE.

JACK KEROUAC

I've come to believe more strongly than ever that after they die, people live on through those who love them.

CAROLINE KENNEDY

WHAT'S SO FASCINATING
AND FRUSTRATING
AND GREAT ABOUT LIFE
IS THAT YOU'RE
CONSTANTLY STARTING
OVER, ALL THE TIME,
AND I LOVE THAT.

BILLY CRYSTAL

YOU'VE GOT TO BUMBLE FORWARD INTO THE UNKNOWN.

FRANK GEHRY

Life's not perfect. Some loose ends may never get trimmed up and tidied.

HODA KOTB

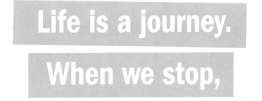

Life is a journey.
When we stop,
things don't go right.

POPE FRANCIS

LIFE IS EITHER A DARING ADVENTURE OR NOTHING.

HELEN KELLER

To achieve great things,
two things are needed:
a plan and not quite
enough time.

LEONARD BERNSTEIN

Man arrives as a novice at each age of his life.

NICOLAS CHAMFORT

If you're not getting happier as you get older, then you're fuckin' up.

ANI DIFRANCO

I HAVE FOUND
THAT IF YOU
LOVE LIFE, LIFE WILL
LOVE YOU BACK.

ARTHUR RUBINSTEIN

TIME
IS THE
SCHOOL
IN WHICH
WE LEARN.

JOAN DIDION

Life is an adventure, it's not a package tour.

ECKHART TOLLE

Don't let yesterday use up
too much of today.

WILL ROGERS

I'm not into nostalgia, and I only look back to find lessons.

IAN SCHRAGER

ALL EXPERIENCE IS GOOD EXPERIENCE.

MEREDITH VIEIRA

They always say
time changes things,
but you actually
have to change them
yourself.

ANDY WARHOL

I have never
regretted
what I did.
I regret things
I didn't do.

INGRID BERGMAN

Old age
is like
everything else.
To make a
success of it,
you've got to
start young.

THEODORE ROOSEVELT

AGED **TO** PERFECTION

We're getting better all the time.
And proud of it.

Sometimes you have to play a long time to be able to play like yourself.

MILES DAVIS

To be seventy years young is sometimes far more cheerful and hopeful than to be forty years old.

OLIVER WENDELL HOLMES

LIVE TO LEARN, AND YOU WILL REALLY LEARN TO LIVE.

JOHN C. MAXWELL

I am my own
experiment.
I am my own
work of art.

MADONNA CICCONE

For the unlearned, old age is winter; for the learned, it is the season of the harvest.

HASIDIC SAYING

THE HEYDAY OF WOMAN'S LIFE IS THE SHADY SIDE OF FIFTY.

ELIZABETH CADY STANTON

141

LIVE A GOOD, HONORABLE LIFE. THEN WHEN YOU GET OLDER AND LOOK BACK, YOU'LL BE ABLE TO ENJOY IT A SECOND TIME.

H. JACKSON BROWN, JR.

The older
I get, the greater
power I seem to
have to help the
world; I am like
a snowball:
The further
I am rolled,
the more I gain.

You come to a point in your life when you really don't care what people think about you, you just care what you think about yourself.

EVEL KNIEVEL

No one can avoid
aging, but aging
productively is
something else.

KATHARINE GRAHAM

The older the fiddler, the sweeter the tune.

IRISH PROVERB

If you get to
my age in life
and nobody
thinks well of you,
I don't care how
big your bank
account is, your
life is a disaster.

One can remain alive
long past the usual date
of disintegration if one
is unafraid of change,
insatiable in intellectual
curiosity, interested in
big things, and happy
in small ways.

EDITH WHARTON

IMMORTALITY
IS A BY-PRODUCT
OF GOOD WORK.

MEL BROOKS

149

My face carries all of my memories. Why would I erase them?

DIANE VON FURSTENBERG

Aging is an extraordinary process where you become the person you should have been.

LOOKING BACK, LOOKING FORWARD

Meditate, ruminate, celebrate—and feel content with who and what you are.

LIFE'S NOT BREATHS YOU TAKE, BUT THE MOMENTS THAT TAKE YOUR BREATH AWAY.

GEORGE STRAIT

A man who
dares to waste
one hour of time
has not discovered
the value of life.

CHARLES DARWIN

Age does not protect you from love. But love, to some extent, protects you from age.

ANAÏS NIN

IT'S BETTER TO BURN OUT THAN TO FADE AWAY.

NEIL YOUNG

EVERY THOUGHT WE THINK
IS CREATING OUR FUTURE.

LOUISE L. HAY

When you're finished changing, you're finished.

BENJAMIN FRANKLIN

Keep your heart
in wonder
at the
daily miracles
of your life.

KHALIL GIBRAN

EVEN THOUGH I GET OLDER,
WHAT I DO NEVER GETS
OLD, AND THAT'S WHAT
I THINK KEEPS ME HUNGRY.

STEVEN SPIELBERG

I'd much rather wear out than rust out.

DAN RATHER

Every man's memory is his private literature.

ALDOUS HUXLEY

Everybody ages.
Everybody dies.
There is no turning
back the clock.
So the question
in life becomes:
What are you
going to do
while you're here?

GOLDIE HAWN

LIFE IS TOO SHORT NOT TO ENJOY IT.

GLEN CAMPBELL

I keep going
because if you
stop, you stop.
Why retire?
Inspire.

MICKEY ROONEY

IF YOU WANT A HAPPY ENDING,
THAT DEPENDS, OF COURSE,
ON WHERE YOU STOP YOUR STORY.

ORSON WELLES

Aging
seems to be
the only
available way
to live
a long time.

DANIEL FRANÇOIS ESPRIT AUBER

When I stand before
God at the end of my life,
I would hope that I would
not have a single bit of
talent left, and could say,
"I used everything you
gave me."

ERMA BOMBECK

I could not at any age be content to take my place in a corner by the fireside and simply look on.

ELEANOR ROOSEVELT

In the seasons
of life, I have
had more than
my share of
summers.

TOM BROKAW

Yes, there's one thing I do want. I want to be aware of the minutes and the seconds, and to make each one count.

JACQUELINE SUSANN

Memories of our lives, of our works, and our deeds will continue in others.

ROSA PARKS